50 WAYS TO HUSTLE YOUR FRIENDS

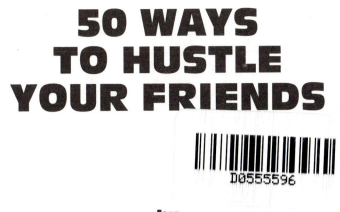

D0555596

by
JIM KAROL

with
Ron Schaffer

Illustrated by
Jeff LeVan

CCC PUBLICATIONS

Published by

CCC Publications
9725 Lurline Avenue
Chatsworth, CA 91311

Manufactured in the United States of America

Cover © 1994 CCC Publications

Interior art & layout by Jeff LeVan

Cover photo by Paul Pelak

Cover models: John Carfi (left) & Jim Karol (right)

Cover/Interior production by Oasis Graphics

ISBN: 0-918259-78-9

If your local U.S. bookstore is out of stock, copies of this book may be obtained by mailing check or money order for $6.99 per book (plus $2.50 to cover postage and handling) to: CCC Publications; 9725 Lurline Avenue, Chatsworth, CA 91311

Pre-publication Edition - 10/94
First Printing - 4/96
Second Printing - 12/99

Introduction

This book is dedicated to the thousands of friends I have made while performing at colleges and universities throughout the United States.

What you will read in this book is the result of 30 years of experience and study in the fields of magic, mental trickery, and general foolishness. I have culled through thousands of effects, hustles, tricks, and bets that I have learned over the years to bring you the absolute BEST "50" proven "greats"- many of which I have used that helped earn me the nickname "Psychic Madman".

The contents of this book are intended for entertainment purposes only. Just like a good practical joke is more fun when played on a friend, so it is with a good "hustle". The "hustles" in this book can provide you with hours of endless fun, or can be used as "ice breakers" when meeting new people. The possibilities are endless!

Most of the effects you will learn are based on the use of mental and scientific trickery and ingenious wit. All of which can be easily accomplished with everyday objects and very little practice.

So good luck and have fun.

Jim "Madman" Karol

-CONTENTS-

INTRODUCTION

CHAPTER ONE - COIN CAPERS & DOLLAR DECEPTIONS

CHAPTER TWO - CARD CONS

CHAPTER THREE - PSYCHIC PSLICKERY

CHAPTER FOUR - SCIENTIFIC CHICANERY

CHAPTER FIVE - HUSTLE HALL OF FAME

CHAPTER SIX - FINALLY A USE FOR MATH

CHAPTER SEVEN - TWO-PERSON SWINDLES

CHAPTER EIGHT - MADMAN'S FAVORITES

Chapter One

Coin Capers and Dollar Deceptions

Money fascinates people. So anytime you involve money in your hustles you will capture peoples' attention immediately. This is a great way to "hook" them. By following the instructions in this chapter you could easily cheat your friends out of their hard earned cash. You know what they say- "A fool and his money are soon parted." Of course, I know you wouldn't do that to your friends. This is all intended for good clean fun. By the way, I need some change, do you have two tens for a five?

THE BILL BET

The Hustle -

This is one of my personal favorite hustles. Have someone remove a five dollar bill from his wallet. Tell him to crumple it up into a ball and place it on the table. You then cover up the bill using an inverted drinking glass or cup. It has to be opaque (that means you can't see through it). Bet your friend five dollars that you can remove that bill from under the cup without touching the cup. Of course this sounds impossible so he is likely to   take you on.

How it's done -

The first thing you want to do is prepare ahead of time before your friend comes into the room. Take a five dollar bill, crumple it up and stick it under the table using double stick tape. If it is impossible to do this ahead of time, simply have a crumpled bill sitting on your lap. Now, set up the situation and make the bet. Make some weird facial expression as if you are straining very hard as you reach under the table directly beneath the cup. Remove the duplicate bill that you stuck there. Then bring your hand out from under the table with the crumpled bill in it and say, "Got it!" Your friend will be so amazed that he will immediately lift up the cup to see if the bill is indeed gone. When HE lifts up the cup, quickly grab his five dollar bill and thank him for it - as you said, YOU didn't touch the cup.

HEADS I WIN, TAILS YOU LOSE

The Hustle -

I love this one. You can offer this as a game (with you always winning, of course) or as a demonstration of your amazing psychic powers. Have a friend place a handful of coins on the table. Any number of coins can be used. Your friend then begins to turn over coins at random while your back is turned. Each time he turns over a coin he calls out, "turn". You tell him he may continue as long as he wishes and the same coin may be turned over as often as desired. When he is done, instruct him to slide any one coin off to the side and cover it with his hand. You turn round and can correctly guess whether the covered coin is heads or tails. This can be repeated as often as he wishes.

How it's done -

It's all done mathematically. Before turning your back, count the number of heads showing on the table. Then turn your back. Each time your friend calls out "turn", add one to this number. If the final total is even, there will be an even number of heads on the table including the one covered. And if the total is odd there will be an odd number of heads. Therefore, it is simple deduction to tell whether the covered coin is heads or tails.

THE TEN-SPOT HUSTLE

The Hustle -
This is a quickie. (Don't get excited, I didn't mean that kind!) Have someone look at a ten dollar bill. Bet him that even though he is looking at the
bill, he can't tell you how many times the word "ten" appears on the ten
dollar bill. Let him look as long as he likes, unless he knows this hustle
he'll always guess wrong.

How it's done -
Most people will guess that the word "ten" appears "11" times. But the
correct answer is "12". Most people overlook the "ten" in the words
"legal <u>ten</u>der". (I knew you'd like this one.)

DIME DILEMMA

The Hustle -

Bet a friend that you can drop a dime from a height of three inches above the table and have it land on its edge. Let him try it a couple of times to see that it is (apparently) impossible.

How it's done -

Wet the side of a tall, straight glass. Simply hold the dime against the glass near the top and drop it. The moisture will hold it against the glass and it will land on the table on its edge. Another bet your friends will hate you for, but try on their own friends.

THE SPIRIT OF '76

The Hustle -
Here's another quickie for you using a dollar bill. Bet your friends that they can't find the date 1776 on a dollar bill.

How it's done -
Most people never find it because it's written in Roman numerals at the base of the pyramid. (Aren't you a stinker!)

Chapter Two

Card Cons

There are more ways to hustle or cheat people with a deck of cards than all other methods combined. Most techniques involve lots of skill and years of practice. However, the card hustles in this chapter require no skill and very little practice. (I knew you'd like that). Learn a few of these and next time your friends invite you over for a friendly game of cards - they'll be in for a few surprises.

DOUBLE CUT FORCE

The Hustle -

For this one you will need a deck of cards. You will have someone choose a card. Instruct them to hold it for a moment with both hands but make sure you do not see it. Have them place the card back in the pack and shuffle them up. You then take the cards and start looking through them one at a time. You explain to your friend that you are searching for their fingerprints on the card they chose. Sure enough, you pick out one card and it is theirs.

How it's done -

This is an example of forcing a card on someone without them realizing it. Choose a card that you want to "force" and place it on top of the deck. Naturally you do this when no one is around. Let's say the top card is the Ace of diamonds. Shuffle the cards but make sure the Ace remains on top. Hand the deck to someone and have them cut about a quarter of the deck and turn that pack face up onto the rest of the cards. Then have them cut the cards again, this time deeper (past the face up pile). They are then to turn that entire packet upside down and replace it onto the deck. This will leave a packet of cards face up on top of the deck. Have them remove all the face up cards and look at the very first face down card. This card will actually be the original top card, the Ace of diamonds. Have them hold onto the card with two hands, supposedly "to get their fingerprints on it". Then tell them to place their card back in the deck and give them a good shuffle. Go through the deck pretending to study the cards for "prints". When you find the Ace of diamonds you say, "Aha! I found your fingerprints on this card!" If you want, you can use a magnifying glass to "dress" this up a bit.

THE SUCKER CARD BET

The Hustle -
Tell your friend that you'd like to show him a card trick. You have him choose a card and replace it in the pack. You then start dealing cards face up onto the table one at a time. You tell your friend that you will use your magic powers to tell him when his card will be the next one turned over. After turning over several cards, you set the rest of the pack on the table and bet your friend that the next card you turn over will be his card. Since he has already seen you pass his card which is lying buried underneath cards face up on the table, he eagerly will bet you thinking that you blew it. You then reach over to a card on the table and turn it over. It's their card. Quickly collect your bet.

How it's done -
While shuffling a deck of cards, get a glimpse of the bottom card. Do not make this obvious. Memorize this card, this is your "key card". (Let's say it's the Ace of Hearts.) With your "key card" on the bottom of the deck, hold the cards in your hand ready for dealing. Start dealing cards one at a time face down onto a pile in front of you. Tell your friend they may call out "stop" any time they want. When they call "stop", you show them the top card from the face down pile on the table, making sure you don't see what it is. You then replace that card face down on top of the pile on the table. You then place the remaining cards in your hand on top of that pile. What this does is place your "key card" (the Ace of Hearts) directly on top of his chosen card. So when you take cards off the top of the deck and lay them face up, one at a time, on the table, you know that their card will be the one immediately following the Ace of Hearts (your key card). But first cut the cards and replace the cut. This will make it look like his card is really lost in the deck. Before you start laying cards face up on the table say to your friend, "I haven't done this trick for a while." This sets them up for the sucker ending. You start flipping cards face up on the table, one at a time, while looking for your "key card". Once you see your "key card", don't stop or even hesitate but continue to

lay down three or four more cards onto the table. Then set the rest of the deck down and say, "I bet you the next card I turn over will be your card." Since he has seen his card pass by and you've set the deck down he assumes that you are going to turn over the next card on the deck.
They will naturally take the bet. After they do, simply reach over to the table and turn over his chosen card to win the bet. Then cover up because this one will get you a deserved smack.

THE CARD CONTEST

The Hustle -

Challenge your friend to a special contest with cards. Give him a deck of cards to shuffle and then spread them face down upon the table. Explain to him how the contest works. You each take turns flipping a card face up, one at a time. The one who turns over the Ace of Spades loses. Loser buys the next round of drinks. Keep your money in your wallet because you will definitely win this one.

How it's done -

First of all, you have a 50-50 chance that you will win without having to cheat. Well, not exactly cheat. Before you pick up each card you turn the card up to peek at it before you turn it over. If you see the Ace of Spades, set it back down and turn over another card. Upon seeing that your friend will loudly protest that the card you peeked at and didn't turn over was the Ace of Spades. You simply say, "No, it wasn't." They will turn that card over to see for themselves. And as soon as they do, they will lose the contest. You see the only rule was the one who turns over the Ace of Spades loses. Remind him to pay closer attention to the rules next time as you enjoy your free drink.

PREMONITION

The Hustle:

A few days before a party or other event, you mail an envelope to a friend with instructions telling them not to open the envelope, and to bring it to the party. Tell them it contains a prediction. During the party or event, you break open a deck of cards and shuffle them. You have your friend who brought the envelope call out a number between 1 and 20. Let's say they call out '7'. You then count down to the seventh card and turn it over for all to see. You then instruct them to open the envelope. Inside they will be amazed to find that you have correctly predicted the turned over card.

How it's done:

If done properly, this effect will boggle their minds. You are going to perform what is known as the "count down force". You are actually going to force them to choose a certain card, even though it appears that they have a free selection. Start by placing the card that you want to force on top of the deck ahead of time. Show the deck to be normal, then shuffle the cards, keeping the top card intact. (To do this just riffle the cards together and drop the top card last.)

Hold the cards in your left hand as though you're ready to deal. When your friend calls out a number, start dealing cards into your right hand, one at a time, on top of each other. What this does is reverse the order of the cards. So if '7' was called, and you counted off seven cards into your hand, the top card (the 'force' card) will now be seventh from the top. Place the packet in your right

hand on top of the packet in your left hand but turn it perpendicular (see illustration). As of yet no one knows what you are going to do, so they won't notice anything. The force card is now seventh from the top. You now turn over the top packet (in this case seven cards), and announce "there is the seventh card." Then have someone open up the envelope to see that your prediction was correct.

POKER HAND BET

The Hustle -
Offer to show your friends a new kind of poker game. Explain that it is played with 10 cards: 3 tens, 3 Queens, 3 Kings and a Jack. Have someone shuffle the cards and spread them out on the table face down. You and a friend take turns picking a card for your hand. When all ten cards are chosen each of you turns them face up and highest poker hand wins. You play this game a couple of times and you win some and you lose some. But as soon as a bet is made, you win every time.

How it's done -
The first thing you need to do is make a mark on the back of the Jack so that you can identify it when the cards are spread out face down. A pencil dot or a scratch works well. Just so it's not obvious. The key to winning the poker hand is to not pick the marked card, the Jack. Because no matter what other cards are chosen, whoever picks the Jack will always loose. Make sure during the crucial betting hand that you pick first so that there is no chance of being stuck with the Jack.

SIDE BY SIDE

The Hustle -

Here's a quick one to do while playing a game of cards. It will have your friends wondering about your "mystical powers". Have someone shuffle the cards thoroughly. Ask someone to call out the values of any two cards (such as "Jack" and "5"). Not the suits - just the values. Put your hand on the deck for a moment and look as if you are contemplating a problem. Then announce that a "Jack" and a "5" will be side by side somewhere in that deck of cards. Your friend looks through the deck and sure enough, there is a "Jack" and a "5" side by side.

How it's done -

There is no trick to this, it just happens automatically. At least 90% of the time, any two cards mentioned (values only) will appear side by side somewhere in a shuffled deck of cards. Try it, you'll be surprised how often this works. About 9% of the time they will be separated by only one card. And about 1% of the time you'll miss altogether. If this happens, blame it on your lack of concentration, and offer to try it again. Chances are extremely slim that it won't work twice in a row.

TELL-TALE DICE

The Hustle -

For this hustle you will need three dice and a deck of cards. For effect, profess to have unusual psychic powers and show your friends a piece of paper with a prediction written on it. Fold the piece of paper and hand it to someone to hold. Have someone shake up the three dice and roll them onto the table. Then have him add up all the numbers showing on top. Then have him turn all the dice upside down and add up all numbers on the faces that were against the table. Have him add both sets of numbers together. Let's say the numbers add up to "21". Have someone count down to the 21st card in the deck and turn it over. When they open up and read your prediction it will be the same as the 21st card. Your amazing prediction has come true.

How it's done -

This works because of the little known fact that the numbers on top and bottom of any die always add up to "7". Therefore, if you add up the numbers on the tops and bottoms of three dice the sum will always be 3 x 7 or "21". It throws people off if you add up all the tops first and then add up all the bottoms. Of course, ahead of time you checked out the 21st card and that's the card you write as your prediction. Once they are amazed at your psychic powers tell them you'll give them tomorrow's winning lottery numbers for $500.

22

QUICK DRAW CARDS

The Hustle -

Remove from a deck of cards the two top cards and show them a black Queen and a black Jack (one spades, the other clubs). Place them face down on the table and invite someone to place both cards, in separate positions, anywhere in the deck. Pick up the deck and give it several riffle shuffles. Those two cards are now lost somewhere in the deck. Bet someone that you can find those two cards and lay them face up on the table by themselves in less than two seconds. Since this sounds impossible they will take that bet.

How it's done -

First of all, this is a con job. What makes this work is the fact that peoples' powers of observation are usually pretty poor. What they don't notice is that the first two cards you showed them are a Jack of spades and a Queen of clubs, but the last two cards that you throw face up onto the table are a Jack of clubs and a Queen of spades. Since these two pairs of cards look alike everyone assumes they were the same pair of cards. To prepare, have your cards set up in advance like this. Place a Queen of spades on the bottom of the deck. On top of the deck place the Jack of clubs; on top of that place the Queen of clubs, and on top of that place the Jack of spades.

TO PERFORM - Take off the two top cards (Qc and Js) and casually show them, but don't call attention to the suits. Simply say, "Here I have a Jack and a Queen." Place them face down on the table and have someone slide them anywhere into the pack. Next, riffle shuffle the cards several times keeping the Queen of spades on the bottom and the Jack of clubs on top (unknown to your audience). After making the bet, hold the deck in one hand and squeeze the deck on top and bottom with your fingers and thumb. When they say "go", quickly slide the top and bottom cards off of the deck and throw them face up onto the table and collect your bet.

LAST CARD WINS

The Hustle -

Here is another unique contest with cards that you can challenge your friends with. To play, you will need 30 cards (or coins if you wish). Each person takes turns picking between one and six cards off of the table. The one who takes the last card wins. Needless to say, you always win!

How it's done -

The secret here is to count the cards as they are being picked up. Make sure you are the one who picks up the 9th, the 16th, and the 23rd card. Since you can pick up anywhere from one to six cards, this should be easy to do. If you happen to miss the 9th card, make sure you pick up the 16th. With a little concentration, you will win every time.

Chapter Three

Psychic Pslickery

It's fun to con your friends into believing that you have psychic powers. Move objects with your mind, predict the future, and read someone's thoughts. These are just some of the things that you will apparently be able to do by following the instructions in this chapter. Of course, it helps if you have gullible friends. Here's a good test. Say to your friend - "Did you know that the word "gullible" is not in the dictionary?" If they say, with a serious look, "Oh, really?" you know they are an easy mark. Go get 'em.

GOOD IMPRESSIONS

The Hustle -

Tell your friend that you would like to test out your recently acquired ability to read minds. Hand him a piece of paper, a pencil, and book to write on. Tell him to think of any city in the United States and to write it down on that piece of paper. You state that writing it down helps him to visualize the image more intensely, which will help you with this experiment. Once that is done, have him fold the paper several times so that no one can read what is written on it. Then have your friend place the piece of paper in his pocket and go into the next room because "you want to see if your telepathy will work through walls." After about 10 seconds you call him back into the room and proceed to correctly name the city written on the piece of paper.

How it's done -

First, you will need to use a hardcover book that has a jacket on it. Unknown to your audience you have secretly placed a sheet of paper and piece of carbon paper under the jacket and taped it in place. Have this book lying around as if it just happened to be there. When he uses the book to write on, the carbon will pick up an impression of the city he wrote. Simply wait till he leaves the room, lift up the jacket, and check out what he wrote. The rest is just showmanship.

THE MYSTERIOUS MARK

The Hustle:
Instruct a volunteer to hold out both hands in front of them, palms facing the floor. Have them place one of their hands at their side, and form a fist with the other. Then draw an outline of an open hand on a piece of paper. Next you reach over to a nearby ashtray and dip your forefinger into the ashes. Touch that same finger to the "palm" of the hand you drew to transfer some ashes onto the paper. Next you crumble the piece of paper, place it in the ashtray, and burn it. Ask your volunteer to slowly open up their hand and turn it over. Mysteriously, a smudge of ashes is found in the center of their palm. (The reason I put this particular effect in this book, this was the very first trick I had played on me, by my dad, and it left a stunning impression which I never forgot).

How it's done:
Before you begin your story, and unknown to everyone else, you dip the tip of your middle finger into some ashes. When you get to the part of your explanation where you tell them to place their hands out in front of them, you grab both hands with yours (see illus.) and say - "raise them just a little," and while lifting their hands simply touch their palm with your middle finger, this will leave a deposit of ashes. By the time you are half way through your story, your volunteer won't even remember you grabbing their hands to do the dirty work.

SERIAL NUMBER PREDICTION

The Hustle -

Have a friend remove a dollar bill from his wallet, crumble it into a tiny ball, and place it onto the table. You remove a handkerchief or napkin from your pocket, unfold it and lay it flat over the crumbled bill. Bet your friends that you can guess the serial number of the crumbled bill. Have someone write down the numbers as you call them out. When you are done, lift up the handkerchief and let the bill roll out onto the table. Let someone straighten out the bill and read off the serial number. It is found that you were 100% correct. As if they had any doubts!

How it's done -

This will require a little boldness on your part but I know you can do it. In advance, memorize the serial number from a dollar bill and crumble it up into a tiny ball in your right hand by pinching a part of it between two fingers. Do not hold your hand stiff. Try to make it look natural. Have someone remove a dollar bill from his wallet and crumble it up. Don't tell him ahead of time what you are going to do so he doesn't look at the serial number. With the crumbled bill on the table, cover it up with a handkerchief or napkin. Call out the serial numbers you memorized. Now comes the tricky part. When you pick up the hanky, pick up his dollar bill along with it and when the hanky is almost off the table let go of the bill hidden in your hand. It will appear as if it's his bill that drops to the table. Stuff his bill along with the hanky in your pocket (or purse) and have him open and read the serial number off the bill on the table. Of course the numbers will match. Practice this a few times so you can do it without being "caught with the goods".

PSYCHOKINESIS

The Hustle -

Here is another way to con your friends into thinking that you have amazing "powers". Place a matchbox on the palm of your hand. Make a motion over the top with your other hand along with a strained facial expression. As everyone looks on, the matchbox begins to move slightly and then rises off of your hand approximately a half an inch apparently under its own power. Upon examining the matchbox it is found that nothing is inside or attached to the box. The only possible explanation is that you have caused the matchbox to move using the power of your mind.

How it's done -

This con is very simple, but what will "sell" this is your acting ability. Have the drawer part way open when you place the matchbox in your hand. When you close the drawer, pinch a bit of your skin in the box. The best place to do this is at the fleshy part at the base of your thumb. Keep your hand slightly cupped while you do this. Now, if you slowly straighten out your hand it will cause the front of the box to rise up. And if viewed from the front is appears as if the box is floating off of your hand.

WORD PREDICTION

The Hustle -

Bet your friends that you can use your "psychic powers" to predict what word will be chosen, at random, from any book.

How it's done -

Even though this will appear to be a random selection, you are really going to "force" the tenth word on page 89 of any book you choose. Naturally, you are going to look up that word and write it down ahead of time. Set that book on a table as if it just happened to be laying nearby so it will look natural to use it. Tell your friend that you wrote a prediction on a piece of paper, and give it to them to hold. Tell them that you are now going to select two numbers at random with their help. You ask them to give you any three digit number and then write it down on a piece of paper. You then reverse those digits and subtract the lower number from the higher. You then reverse those digits and add them to your answer (see example). You tell your friend that the last two digits will indicate the page number (89), and the first two digits will determine which word will be used by counting that number of words from the top of the page (10). When they read off that word, they will find that it matches your prediction. Follow this example with any three digit number and your answer will always be 1089. Therefore you simply "predict" the tenth word on page 89 of your book.

any three digit number	782	495
reverse and subtract	- 287	+594...reverse and add
	495	1089...answer

X MARKS THE SPOT

The Hustle -
Here is another demonstration of psychic phenomena. Present to your friends a magazine, a felt tip pen, and a folded piece of paper. Explain that on the piece of paper you wrote a prediction. Set it in full view of everyone. Hand someone the magazine and tell them to hold it behind their back. Instruct them to open it up somewhere in the center. Hand them the felt marker and tell them to reach behind their back and, without looking, place a small "x" somewhere near the center of the page. Have them close the magazine and hand it to you. Hand the magazine to someone and have them look through it until they find the page with the "x". Have them read off the word that the "x" goes through. When the piece of paper is opened up, it is found that your prediction matches the word "x"ed out in the magazine.

How it's done -
Prepare for this one ahead of time by placing an "x" through a word near the center of any page approximately in the middle of the magazine. Write this word on a piece of paper and fold it up – this is your prediction. Next, leave a felt tip marker out a day or two without the cap on so it dries out and will not mark. Naturally when they follow your instructions and attempt to make the mark in the magazine, nothing will happen. So when someone looks through the magazine, the only mark they'll find is the "x" you placed there ahead of time (you clever devil, you).

DATE BAIT

The Hustle -

Here is a quick way to get a free lunch or drink. Have your friend reach into his pocket and remove a coin but keep it hidden from view in his fist. You then make this statement, "Although neither of us can see that coin, I'll bet you I can tell you the date." Hopefully, he'll take that bet.

How it's done -

After he agrees to your bet, you simply say, "The date is March 10, 1995" or whatever today's date is. Remember, you said, "...I can tell you the date," and you did. I know it's corny but it works.

Chapter Four

Scientific Chicanery

Because most people weren't paying close attention during science class it's very easy to fool them by knowing a few unusual scientific principles. The effects in this chapter are very visual and a lot of fun to do. So don't feel guilty if you successfully sucker your friends by using the hustles included here, after all, it's not your fault they weren't paying closer attention in school.

HIGH AND DRY

The Hustle -

Place a penny on a plate and also pour a small amount of water onto the plate. Enough to cover the penny completely. Challenge your friends to remove the penny without getting their fingers wet, without touching the plate, and without using any implements to touch the coin. (And of course they can't wait 24 hours for the water to evaporate.) When they give up, bet them that you can do it. If you can, they buy lunch, and if you can't do it then you'll treat. Don't worry, your money is safe–read on.

How it's done -

All you have to do is crumble up a piece of paper or a napkin, light it with a match and then drop it onto the plate. Immediately cover the burning paper with an inverted drinking glass. You'll find that the water gets sucked up into the glass leaving the penny high and dry. Simply pick it up and collect your bet.

BALLOON AND GLASS STUNT

The Hustle -
Blow up a small balloon and bet your friend that you can pick up a drinking glass using the inflated balloon. Tell him that you are simply going to touch the balloon to the mouth of the glass and will be able to pick it up. Give him a chance to try it first. After he's failed, you show him how it is done - for a free drink of course.

How it's done -
All you have to do is light a match and drop it into the glass. Immediately place the balloon over the mouth of the glass. The match will go out and the balloon will get sucked into the glass far enough for you to pick up the glass by holding onto the balloon only. Try this, this is really cool. For an explanation of the scientific principle which allows this to work - ask someone smarter than I am.

HIGH STRUNG

The Hustle -
This is a good one to do in a barroom or restaurant, or anywhere there are drinks with ice cubes in them. Tear a strip of paper napkin approximately one inch wide and eight to ten inches long. Tie a small loop into one end just barely large enough to fit over an ice cube in your drink. Challenge someone to use this lasso to pull an ice cube out of the glass. He cannot touch the ice cubes with his fingers or utensils. Several attempts will prove to your friends that this seems like an impossible task. Naturally, you bet everyone that you can do it.

How it's done -
Lay the flat end (opposite the lasso) on top of any ice cube and then sprinkle a good amount of salt over the top. A layer of ice will melt and refreeze. After about 30 - 40 seconds you'll be able to lift the ice cube out of the glass.

BOTTLE AND BALLOON BET

The Hustle -
Hand someone a beer or soda bottle and a long balloon. Challenge them to blow up the balloon inside the bottle. No matter how hard they try they will find it impossible to do. Of course, you bet them that you can do the impossible.

How it's done -
When someone places a balloon in the neck of a bottle and starts to inflate it, the balloon itself seals the opening and prevents air from leaving the bottle and thus makes it impossible for the balloon to be blown up inside the bottle. The way to do it is to place the balloon into the neck of the bottle and then slide a straw into the bottle alongside of the balloon. This will allow the air to escape and you can then inflate the balloon inside the bottle. To really drive your friends nuts, first leave the room so they can't see what you're doing, slide the straw out when finished and return with the balloon inflated in the bottle.

CHAPTER FIVE

Hustle Hall Of Fame

Puzzles are the oldest form of hustles. Ever since cave people drew on cave walls they were trying to trick each other with puzzles. There is even recorded evidence of the famous "cups and balls" hustle depicted on the inner walls of the ancient pyramids in Egypt. Many of the puzzles in the following chapter have been passed down through generations. I'm now passing them along to you. Have fun.

•

THE CONFUSING CUPS

The Hustle -

Place three empty glasses in a row, the middle glass mouth up, the other two mouth down. Challenge your friends to repeat what you are about to do. Take the two glasses at the left (A and B), one in each hand, and turn them over. Next, turn over the two glasses on each end (A and C). Finally, turn over the two left glasses again (A and B) so now all three glasses are sitting on the table with their mouths up. Say, "That is the challenge, by turning over two glasses at a time, turn all three mouths up in three moves, just like I did." Turn the middle glass (B) mouth down and let someone try it. But make sure he bets you first because it will be impossible for him to do.

How it's done -

What makes this impossible for your friend to do is the arrangement of the glasses when he begins. No one notices it is different from when you began. Check out the paragraph above again. When you began there were two glasses mouth down, but when you set it up for him to begin there is only one cup mouth down (B). Even if he remembers and follows your moves exactly, he will end up with all three glasses mouth down instead of up.

A   B   C

YOU
START

A   B   C

FINISH

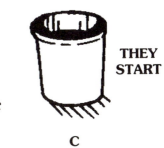

A   B   C

THEY
START

MATCH STICK PUZZLER

The Hustle -
Here is another match stick puzzle that you can have fun with. Arrange
16 matches to form a pattern as in figure 1. The object is to move two
matches to make four squares of the same size.

How it's done -
Move the two matches as indicated in figure 2. After you demonstrate the
solution, you can really confuse your friends by setting it up for them in
"upside down" fashion as in figure 3.

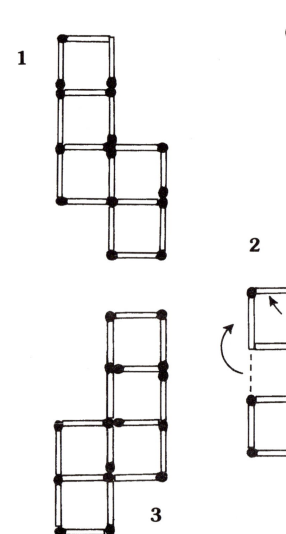

1

2

3

SIX GLASS CHALLENGE

The Hustle -

Arrange six glasses as in figure 1. Three are empty and three are full. Challenge someone to move only one glass and create an arrangement of alternating full and empty glasses.

How it's done -

Most people overlook the most obvious solution. Simply pick up glass number 2 and pour its contents into glass number 5 and then set it back down where it was. This leaves the glasses alternately full and empty.

Figure 1

Figure 2

TRIANGLE TROUBLE

The Hustle -
Challenge your friend to form four triangles of equal size using only six matches or toothpicks.

How it's done -
What makes this so hard for people to figure out is because most people are thinking of a two dimensional figure. But the solution to the puzzle is three dimensional, as illustrated in the following drawing. Lean three matches against each other in "tent" fashion and then lay down the other three matches to connect the base.

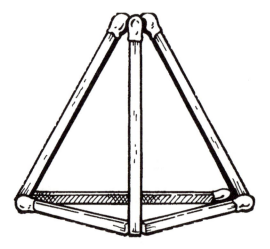

TOOTHPICK TEASER

The Hustle -

Here is a quick puzzle challenge that uses matches or toothpicks. Challenge someone to form three squares using eight toothpicks. Bet him a drink that he can't do it.

How it's done -

Chances are, that if your friend hasn't seen this puzzle before he won't figure it out. So your bet is pretty safe. Here is the simple solution:

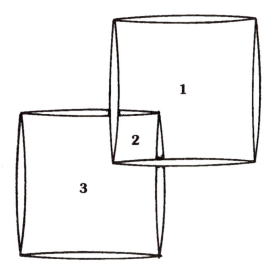

CHAPTER SIX

Finally, A Use For Math

When I was in school my Math teachers were trying to convince me that learning Math would be a useful benefit to me some day. Well, they were right! Hustling and entertaining people with my Math skills has been very beneficial - not to mention fun. I guarantee that you too, will have a lot of fun with the information taught in this chapter. And you don't have to be a math genius to use it.

THE MYSTERIOUS NUMBER NINE

The Hustle -

This one can be done with or without a calculator. Have someone write down any three digit number. Then have them multiply that number by 18. They are then to circle any digit, except zero, in the answer. Ask them to read off, in any order the rest of the digits, even if they are repeated. You then concentrate intensely and correctly name the digit that was circled.

How it's done -

This is another one of those mathematical gems that I don't even question—I just have fun with it. This will work with a three digit or a four digit number. No matter what number they pick, always give them a multiple of "9" to multiply it by. I usually use "18". If you multiply "18" times any number, the digit in the answer will always add up to a multiple of 9. (9, 18, 27, ...). To figure out which digit in the answer is circled simply add up the rest of the numbers that are given to you and subtract that number from the next highest multiple of 9. Your answer will be the circled number. (see example below)

Number written down...452

Multiplied by 18...   x18
                        ————

Answer...   8136

Number circled...   ⑧1 3 6

Sum of other numbers...1+3+6=10

Subtract 10 from next highest multiple of 9 (18)...18 - 10 = 8

8 is the circled number

(You cannot have them circle a zero—it won't always work. If the sum of the other numbers equals a multiple of 9, then you know the number they circled is a "9")

LONG DISTANCE TELEPATHY

The Hustle -
Convincing someone that you have incredible psychic powers is even more believable if you can do it over the phone. Here is a great example. While talking to a friend on the phone have him shuffle a deck of cards. Have him pick any card and turn it over but not to tell you what it is. Next, have him assign that card a number according to its value. (i.e. Ace is 1, two is 2, three is 3,...Jack is 11, Queen is 12, and King is 13.) Next have him add the next higher number to his card. (If he picked a King of Spades, he would add 14 making the total 27.) Have him multiply that result by 5. (In this case the answer would be 135.) Tell your friend that we are going to use the bridge value of the suites: Clubs = 6, Hearts = 7, Diamonds = 8, and Spades = 9. Have him add the value of the suit to his total. (135 + 9 = 144). Finally, have him tell you the result and you immediately tell him the card and the suit he picked.

How it's done -
All you have to do is subtract 5 from your friend's answer. The first figure tells you the card and the second figure tells you the suit (according to the values of the suits listed above).

In our example the result was 144. Subtract 5 = 139, 13 = King and 9= Spades. It's incredible. I wish I knew how it worked.

DICE DECEPTION

The Hustle -

While your back is turned have someone roll three dice. Your friend silently multiplies the number on the first die by 2, then adds 5, and then multiplies that result by 5, then adds the face of the second die, multiplies that result by 10, and finally adds the number on the third die. Your friend then announces the final result. You then amaze everyone by naming the numbers on the faces of all three dice.

How it's done -

This is totally awesome. I'm still not sure how it works but it does. All you have to do is subtract 250 from the final result. The three figures in your answer are the three faces of the dice, in order. Guard this secret well. You'll have a lot of fun fooling your friends.

DIGIT DILEMMA

The Hustle -

Here's a great stunt to pull on anyone using a calculator. Have him punch in the number 12,345,679 (notice the 8 is omitted). Ask your friend which of those digits is his favorite. Let's say he says number "7". Give him another number to multiply times 12,345,679 and when he gets the answer it is all 7's (777,777,777). This will work for any number he picks.

How it's done -

Whatever number he picks as his favorite, you simply multiply that number by 9 in your head and give him that "answer" to use to multiply times 12,345,679. It will always come out as all the same digits. (In the example he picked 7, 7 x 9 = 63, tell him to multiply 63 x 12,345,679.)

DOUBLE CROSS

The Hustle -

Hand someone a piece of paper that is folded several times and tell him that you have written a prediction on it. Next you show him a chart with 16 numbers on it. (See illustration.) Have him circle any number he wants. After he circles a number, you take your pencil and draw a line through all the numbers that are in the same vertical and horizontal rows as that chosen number. Have your friend circle another number that is not crossed out and you repeat what you did the first time. This continues until all the numbers are circled or crossed out. Remind him that he has several free selections during this process. Next have him add up all the circled numbers and then open up your prediction. He will find that both numbers are the same.

How it's done -

These math things drive me crazy. I love them but have no idea how they work. Believe it or not, no matter what numbers are circled, as long as you proceed as stated above, the circled numbers will always add up to 34. Try it and see.

1	2	3	4
5	6	7	8
9	10	11	12
13	14	15	16

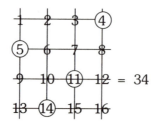 = 34

56

AWE-SUM

The Hustle -
Cut out or tear five pieces of paper. On the first piece write the number "1" on one side and "2" on the other. On the second piece write "3" on one side and "4" on the other. Do the same with "5/6", "7/8", and "9/10". Give the five pieces to someone and have them mix them up while your back is turned. They can turn each piece over or mix them any way they please. Ask them to lay all the pieces on the table and spread them out so the numbers show. Have them tell you how many odd numbers are showing. You then tell them the total sum of all the numbers showing.

How it's done -
All you have to do is subtract the number of odd pieces showing from 30 and this will give you the total sum of all the pieces showing. So if there are 2 odd pieces showing, the sum total of all the pieces showing will be 28. (I should have paid closer attention in Math class cuz I haven't got a clue how this works).

IT FIGURES!

The Hustle -

Bet someone that they can't add up four 4-digit numbers in their head. When they agree to the bet read off these four numbers for him to add mentally. Give the numbers to him one at a time so he can add up the sums as you read off the numbers. The numbers are:

1040

1020

1030

1010

You will win this bet about nine out of ten times.

How it's done -

You'll have to try this on a few friends to see how deceptive it can be. Because of the configuration of the digits and the sequence, most people will give the total as 5000. But the real answer is 4,100.
Try it, you'll like it.

MATH HOAX

The Hustle -

Tell your friend you have a cool mathematical trick to show him. Bet him that he can't figure out how it is done. Tell him to place a penny in one hand and a nickel in the other, but not to let you see which coin is in what hand. Next, tell him to multiply the value of the coin in the left hand by 14. Then have him multiply the value of the coin in the right hand by 14. Then have him add those two numbers together and give you the answer. When he tells you, announce that you now know that he is holding the nickel in his right hand and the penny in his left. (Or vice versa if that is the case.)

How it's done -

Although you present this as a mathematical trick just to throw him off, it is really an exercise in observation. Because it will take longer for some-one to multiply 14 x 5 (value of nickel) in his mind than 14 x 1 (value of penny), you simply notice which "hand" takes him longer to multiply and that's the one with the nickel.

CHAPTER SEVEN

Two-Person Swindles

Hustling others with a friend is twice the fun. It's great having someone else "in on it" with you. Plus you can accomplish things that would simply be impossible to do on your own. In the following chapter are the best two person hustles ever developed. So grab your favorite "partner in crime" and have fun.

TIME TELEPATHY

The Hustle -

Have someone remove his watch, pull out the stem and set the time to any hour he chooses. He is to keep the face of the watch away from you so that you cannot see it. He then passes the watch around so everyone except you knows the hour at which it was set. The last person to view the watch places it face down on the table. Even though you could not see the face of the watch, you correctly name the hour at which it was set.

How it's done -

The last person to view the watch is your accomplice. Both of you envision an imaginary clock on the table. Your helper sets the watch down with the stem of the watch pointing to the correct "hour". If the stem is pointing to your helper, that is "12 noon". Use that as your guide and it should be easy for him to signal you with the correct hour on the watch.

SPOON PICTURES

The Hustle -

At a gathering of friends, tell them you would like to demonstrate a unique talent that you learned from a Madam Babushka while traveling through the Ukraine last Summer. (If they swallow that one, tell them that you have some ocean-front property in Arizona that you'd like to sell them.) Tell your friends that when you leave the room someone is supposed to hold up a spoon in front of his face and stare at it for at least 5 seconds. You tell them that this will take a "picture" of the person's "aura" which will stay on the spoon for several minutes. When he is done, he is to place the spoon in the center of the table and knock on the door for you to return to the room. When you come back in the room you pick up the spoon and stare intently into the bowl. After several seconds you correctly name the chosen person.

How it's done -

No, the spoon is not pointing to the chosen person, that would be too obvious. Instead, your secret accomplice is standing (or sitting) in exactly the same position as the chosen person. Check this out as soon as you come back into the room so that when you pick up the spoon you don't have to look at anyone.

TWO PERSON CARD HUSTLE

The Hustle -

While playing cards ask your friends if they know that you can read minds if the mental energy is focused properly. When you're greeted with puzzled looks offer to demonstrate. Arrange nine cards face up on the table and tell someone to point to a card when your back is turned. After that is done, once again face your friends. Ask someone to touch all nine cards one at a time so everyone is "focusing their mental energies on the same card at the same time." After that is done you correctly name the chosen card. This may be repeated over and over again.

How it's done -

Of course, unknown to everyone else, you are working with a partner on this one. Your partner is going to signal you using a devilishly deceptive method. First, arrange nine cards face up on the table. Put four cards on each side of any 9 spot card. (See illustration.) The 9 spot card is the signal card. After a card is chosen (pointed to when your back is turned), you face the cards and have your partner touch each of the cards with their forefinger one at a time to "help the group focus their mental energies on the chosen card." (Yeah right!) Your partner will touch the "9" card last. Watch very carefully which "pip" on the 9 card is touched. That will tell you which card was chosen. For example, if the upper right hand "pip" was touched, you know that the upper right hand card was chosen. You see, the nine pips on the card are in the same configuration as the nine cards on the table. So each "pip" corresponds to a card on the table. If the 9 card itself is chosen, your partner would touch the center "pip" on the 9 card. Since your friends don't know you're working with a partner, let alone a signaling method, they'll have to conclude that you are "reading the focused energy of their minds." Milk it for all it's worth.

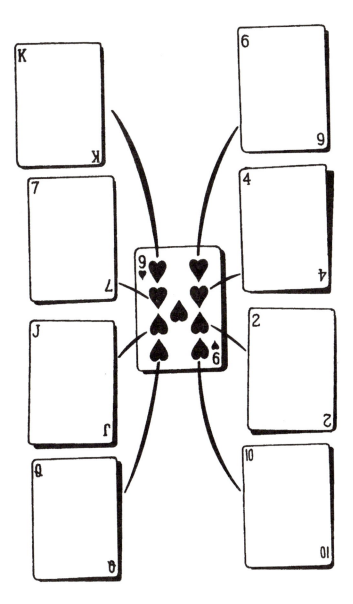

THE COIN CON

The Hustle -

If after doing the "two person card hustle", your audience still doubts your mental prowess, offer this demonstration as additional proof of your ability. Have someone collect four coins, a penny, nickel, dime and quarter. (If your friends are all unemployed college students this may be tough.) While your back is turned have someone place one of the coins under a paper or Styrofoam cup so it can't be seen and place the remaining coins in his pocket. You then use your "mental prowess" to correctly guess which coin is hidden under the cup. You can repeat this as often as you like.

How it's done -

Of course, once again, your secret partner is going to provide a signal for you when they place the cup upside down over the coin. Unknown to everyone else there is a small "nick" on the bottom edge of the cup (made by your fingernail). Your partner and you will use the "clock system" using the "nick" as the "hour hand". Thus if the "nick" is at 12 o'clock (from where you are standing) then the coin hidden beneath is a penny. If the "nick" is turned to 3 o'clock then the coin is a nickel; turned to 6 o'clock, it is a dime. At 9 o'clock, it is a quarter.
Isn't it fun to fool people?

EASY HUSTLE

The Hustle -

Here is a hustle that is a lot of fun to do with a partner. Tell your friends that you are going to leave the room and while you're gone to chose any object in the room. When you return, you will attempt to use your telepathic powers to figure out what object the group chose. You leave the room while they decide on an object and when you return someone begins to name objects in the room one at a time. When he names the chosen object you are able to identify it correctly.

How it's done -

This one is easy. You and your secret partner simply decide on a code to use. A good one is this. Your partner begins to name objects in the room at random and the very next object that he names after a black colored object is the one that the group chose. Another code could be the very next object mentioned after an object named with the letter "C" is mentioned. There are hundreds of possible codes to use. All you have to do is decide upon one to use in advance with your partner.

CHAPTER EIGHT

Madman's Favorites

The following hustles in this chapter have been included for one of two reasons. Either they are some of my personal favorites - or they have helped me earn my nickname, "The Madman." You have to be a little "crazy" to do some of these, but then again, who wants to be normal?

THE YOLK'S ON YOU

(NOTE: Make sure you do this in your friend's house!)

The Hustle -
Tell your friend (or enemy) that you have two magic tricks to show them. First you will make an egg disappear, then the change in their front pocket. Get a raw egg and then open any door that has three hinges on it. Tell your friend to reach through the crack in the door above the center hinge and hold on to the egg. Once they have a hold of the egg, tell them that if they reach into their pocket with their free hand and give you all of their change, you will help them out of their predicament.

How it's done -
At this point they are at your mercy. They can't pull the egg through the crack and because of the hinge, they can't lower their hand to the floor. If they let go of the egg, it will splatter on THEIR floor. They either part with the money or you simply walk away leaving them stranded.

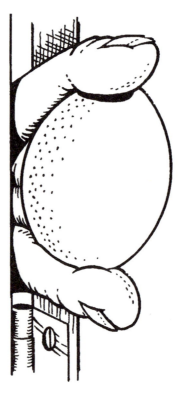

Hot Head

The Hustle:
Explain to your friends that you can cause an object to become hot simply by using the power of your mind. Tell them you will demonstrate by using a piece of gum wrapper foil. Place a piece of the gum wrapper foil on your friend's forehead. Tell him to think of heat, intense heat, tell him you will use your "powers" to heat the foil. Believe it or not, your friend will rip the foil from his head and you will look like a million bucks.

WARNING: Make sure your volunteer has a good sense of humor, or you may get sued for that million bucks.

How it's done:
You are not going to believe how this works until you try it on yourself. Go to the store and buy a pack of cinnamon gum (the popular kind in the big, red package, works best.) Use a piece of foil from one of the sticks, lick the inside of the foil, or dip it in water, then slap it on your subject's forehead and in about 30 to 40 seconds you will look like a miracle worker. (The cinnamon from the gum reacts when wet causing the foil to get hot and tingly.)

THIRD DEGREE BURN

The Hustle -

This is a great follow-up to the previous hustle. Tell someone you can actually cause any object to become hot just by mental powers alone. Pick out some object such as a spoon and lay it on the table in front of you. Show both your hands to be empty. Wave your one hand over the spoon in a very mysterious manner. After a couple of seconds announce that the object is now very hot to the touch. Attempt to pick up the object and scream in pain as you drop it. Immediately show your right forefinger. It has a blister on it. A blister that wasn't there a moment ago when you showed your hands empty.

How it's done -

Most of this hustle is done using your acting ability. The "blister" effect is accomplished by pressing the tip of your forefinger against the hole that is found on the end of a key. Have a key lying on your lap. After you show your hands empty place your right hand on your lap while your left hand is making a motion above the object. While your hand is on your lap it is very easy to pick up the key and press your forefinger against the hole because everyone will be watching your left hand and the object. You then reach for the object with your right hand, drop it, and show your "blister". If someone touches the object immediately after you do and doesn't feel any heat, tell him because you have lost your concentration on the object, it no longer retains any heat.

UNCANNY PREDICTION

The Hustle -

Once again you attempt to demonstrate your awesome psychotic, er, I mean psychic abilities. Write a prediction on a piece of paper and give it to someone to hold. Then hand a deck of cards to someone and instruct him to shuffle the pack. Once that is done tell him to take two cards at a time off the top of the deck and look at them. If both cards are red, he keeps them; if both cards are black, he gives them to you and if one is red and one is black, he puts them in the center. Have him go through the entire deck like this and when completed have him count up his red cards and then you count up your black cards. It is found that he has two more cards than you do. When your prediction is opened and read its says, "You will have two more cards than I do." You then repeat this process with a different outcome yet you are still able to accurately predict what will happen. Uncanny!

How it's done -

This works because of an incredible mathematical principle. If you take a regular deck of 52 cards, shuffle them up, and then remove pairs of cards and separate them according to the instructions above, you will always be left with the same number of cards in the "red" pile as there are in the "black" pile. Try it. It always works that way. But you don't want people to suspect that, so what you do is leave two black cards behind in the card box (unknown to anyone, of course). You then write the prediction, "You'll have two more cards than I do." Because that is the way it will turn out if two black cards are missing. You then place the cards back in the box thus adding the two missing black cards to the pack. You then have your friend try it again. This time your prediction will be, "You will have the same number of cards that I have."
Because, with a full deck, that is what the outcome will be, thus making your second prediction correct. Are you awesome or what?

THE POOL HUSTLE

The Hustle:

Here's a great hustle to pull on your friend while playing a game of pool. Place two balls up against the cushion, touching each other as in figure #1. Place the "8" ball on top of the cushion held in place by the other two balls. (see figure 2)

Spot the cue ball as if you were going to "break". Bet your friend that you can hit the "8" ball with the cue ball without hitting either of the other two balls. Of course this looks impossible.

How it's done:

Line the cue ball up with the eight ball and take a nice soft shot towards the 8 ball. While following through, accidently bump the table with your thigh. This will cause the 8 ball to fall off the ledge and roll over the other two balls in line with your shot. (fig. 3) Practice this a few times to get the timing down. (Even if your friend catches you bumping the table you still win the bet).

1

2

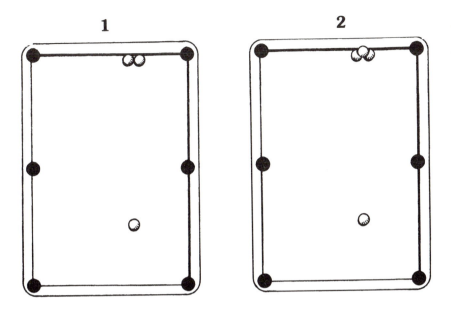

3

STRENGTH CHALLENGE

The Hustle:

Here is a challenge that appears to be a feat of strength. Tell someone to make two fists and place one on top of the other. (see illus.) Tell them to hold their fists together as tight as they can, because you are going to attempt to knock their fists apart using only two fingers of each hand. No matter how hard they press their fists together, you will be able to easily separate them by slapping them with two fingers of each hand. Then you challenge them to try to knock your fists apart using only two fingers from each hand. No matter how hard they try, they find it impossible to do.

How it's done:

No matter how hard someone tries to keep their fists together, they will find even a child can knock them apart. So why is it impossible to knock

yours apart? You cheat, of course. Unknown to them, when you place one fist on top of the other, you secretly place your thumb of your bottom hand into your upper fist and hold it tightly. As long as they are only using two fingers from each hand, it will be impossible for them to separate your fists.

THE BOTTOM DEAL HUSTLE

The Hustle:

I saved the best for last. Here's a great way to con your friends into thinking you're a card shark. Tell them you're going to demonstrate how to deal a winning hand in poker using what professional gamblers call, "the bottom deal". You proceed to deal five face down poker hands. When you are done, you turn over the hand dealt to yourself and show the hand to be four kings. Your friends complain that they saw you deal the cards from the bottom of the deck when it was time to give yourself a card. You explain that you made it obvious for demonstration purposes only. Gather up the cards and tell them you will proceed to do the bottom deal again, this time without being noticed. Tell them they will swear all the cards will be seen to come off the top of the deck. Openly place the four kings on the bottom of the deck, and re-deal the five hands, this time removing every card from the top. When finished, ask if anyone saw you dealing from the bottom. When they say no, you then tell them that you dealt from the middle of the deck, and gave yourself a better hand. Then turn your hand over revealing that you now have four aces.

(This seems long and complicated, but try it and you'll see that it is easy to do and very very strong.)

How it's done:

Don't worry, you do not need to spend weeks or months practicing "bottom" or "middle" deals. This is actually quite easy. You prepare for this ahead of time by placing the four kings on the bottom of a deck of cards. Do this right in front of your friends. What they do not know, is that you secretly placed the four aces on top of the deck ahead of time. When you deal the five hands the first time, the fifth hand is dealt to yourself. Deal the cards from the top, but every time you come to yourself, deliberately take the bottom card, which will be a king. After dealing all five hands, show your hand to be the four kings. As you pick up the cards to apparently do it again, you take the hand to your left (face down), and one at a time place the four hands on top of each other and your hand with the kings goes on the bottom of the deck. Now as you deal the hands the second time, (all from the top) you will automatically receive the four aces, and look like a card shark. (This happens because the aces were distributed evenly the first time you dealt the hands.)

ABOUT THE AUTHOR

JIM KAROL (Psychic Madman)

Jim picked up the name "Psychic Madman" in 1990. The "Psychic" portion of the name came from correctly predicting several State Daily Lottery Numbers. The largest was in Pennsylvania on December 22, 1990, when Jim told everyone at his shows to play 222, and over 12 million dollars was won. The "Madman" part of the name comes from the chain saws, knives, staple guns, and various other objects that Jim uses while performing at hundreds of colleges and universities yearly. Besides performing one of the wildest shows in the country, Jim is probably best known for his after-show activities, where he teaches some of his tricks of the trade and demonstrates some of his more bizarre skills, such as sticking his fingers in a wolf trap, and bending 60 penny nails in his bare hands.

Jim has taught courses at several universities, and has been studying magic for over 30 years. One of his strongest assets is his B.S. in BS.

*Jim is also in the Guinness book of Records, for being the world record holder in throwing a playing card 201 feet.

Special thanks to Ron Schaffer...

Ron is a professional magician, writer, entrepreneur, and teacher. Armed with a bachelors degree in education and over 30 years experience in the art of illusion, he is one of the foremost magic instructors in the country. Ron is the creator of the "Learn At Home Magic" video series which is sold nationally. He is the inventor of several magic effects which are manufactured and sold to other magicians. Ron offers magic supplies, books, and video tapes through his mail order business. For information write to: Ron's Magic, P.O. Box 8807, Dept. H, Allentown, PA 18105

& Jeff LeVan

Jeff's first commercial cartooning job was at age 10, when he drew and marketed his own successful line of greeting cards. His ability to animate inanimate objects and animals has its roots in his childhood love of 1930's and 1940's classic cartoons. This passion has led him to his present career as owner of Jeff LeVan's Kustom Kartoons in Bethlehem, PA, where he specializes in logo and package design for candy, toys and gag gifts, as well as motor sports.

TITLES BY CCC PUBLICATIONS

Retail $4.99
POSITIVELY PREGNANT
SIGNS YOUR SEX LIFE IS DEAD
WHY MEN DON'T HAVE A CLUE
40 AND HOLDING YOUR OWN
CAN SEX IMPROVE YOUR GOLF?
THE COMPLETE BOOGER BOOK
THINGS YOU CAN DO WITH A USELESS MAN
FLYING FUNNIES
MARITAL BLISS & OXYMORONS
THE VERY VERY SEXY ADULT DOT-TO-DOT BOOK
THE DEFINITIVE FART BOOK
THE COMPLETE WIMP'S GUIDE TO SEX
THE CAT OWNER'S SHAPE UP MANUAL
PMS CRAZED: TOUCH ME AND I'LL KILL YOU!
RETIRED: LET THE GAMES BEGIN
MALE BASHING: WOMEN'S FAVORITE PASTIME
THE OFFICE FROM HELL
FOOD & SEX
FITNESS FANATICS
YOUNGER MEN ARE BETTER THAN RETIN-A
BUT OSSIFER, IT'S NOT MY FAULT

Retail $4.95
1001 WAYS TO PROCRASTINATE
THE WORLD'S GREATEST PUT-DOWN LINES
HORMONES FROM HELL II
SHARING THE ROAD WITH IDIOTS
THE GREATEST ANSWERING MACHINE MESSAGES OF ALL TIME
WHAT DO WE DO NOW?? (A Guide For New Parents)
HOW TO TALK YOU WAY OUT OF A TRAFFIC TICKET
THE BOTTOM HALF (How To Spot Incompetent Professionals)
LIFE'S MOST EMBARRASSING MOMENTS
HOW TO ENTERTAIN PEOPLE YOU HATE
YOUR GUIDE TO CORPORATE SURVIVAL
THE SUPERIOR PERSON'S GUIDE TO EVERYDAY IRRITATIONS
GIFTING RIGHT

TITLES BY CCC PUBLICATIONS

Blank Books ($3.99)
GUIDE TO SEX AFTER BABY
GUIDE TO SEX AFTER 30
GUIDE TO SEX AFTER 40
GUIDE TO SEX AFTER 50
GUIDE TO SEX AFTER MARRIAGE

Retail $4.95 – $4.99
"?" book
LAST DIET BOOK YOU'LL EVER NEED
CAN SEX IMPROVE YOUR GOLF?
THE COMPLETE BOOGER BOOK
FLYING FUNNIES
MARITAL BLISS & OXYMORONS
THE ADULT DOT-TO-DOT BOOK
THE DEFINITIVE FART BOOK
THE COMPLETE WIMP'S GUIDE TO SEX
THE CAT OWNER'S SHAPE UP MANUAL
THE OFFICE FROM HELL
FITNESS FANATICS
YOUNGER MEN ARE BETTER THAN RETIN-A
BUT OSSIFER, IT'S NOT MY FAULT
YOU KNOW YOU'RE AN OLD FART WHEN...
1001 WAYS TO PROCRASTINATE
HORMONES FROM HELL II
SHARING THE ROAD WITH IDIOTS
THE GREATEST ANSWERING MACHINE MESSAGES
WHAT DO WE DO NOW??
HOW TO TALK YOU WAY OUT OF A TRAFFIC TICKET
THE BOTTOM HALF
LIFE'S MOST EMBARRASSING MOMENTS
HOW TO ENTERTAIN PEOPLE YOU HATE
YOUR GUIDE TO CORPORATE SURVIVAL
NO HANG-UPS (Volumes I, II & III – $3.95 ea.)
TOTALLY OUTRAGEOUS BUMPER-SNICKERS ($2.95)

Retail $5.95
30 – DEAL WITH IT!
40 – DEAL WITH IT!
50 – DEAL WITH IT!
60 – DEAL WITH IT!
OVER THE HILL – DEAL WITH IT!
SLICK EXCUSES FOR STUPID SCREW-UPS
SINGLE WOMEN VS. MARRIED WOMEN
TAKE A WOMAN'S WORD FOR IT
SEXY CROSSWORD PUZZLES
SO, YOU'RE GETTING MARRIED
YOU KNOW HE'S A WOMANIZING SLIMEBALL WHEN...
GETTING OLD SUCKS
WHY GOD MAKES BALD GUYS
OH BABY!
PMS CRAZED: TOUCH ME AND I'LL KILL YOU!
WHY MEN ARE CLUELESS
THE BOOK OF WHITE TRASH
THE ART OF MOONING
GOLFAHOLICS
CRINKLED 'N' WRINKLED
SMART COMEBACKS FOR STUPID QUESTIONS
YIKES! IT'S ANOTHER BIRTHDAY

SEX IS A GAME
SEX AND YOUR STARS
SIGNS YOUR SEX LIFE IS DEAD
MALE BASHING: WOMEN'S FAVORITE PASTIME
THINGS YOU CAN DO WITH A USELESS MAN
MORE THINGS YOU CAN DO WITH A USELESS MAN
RETIREMENT: THE GET EVEN YEARS
LITTLE INSTRUCTION BOOK OF THE RICH & FAMOUS
WELCOME TO YOUR MIDLIFE CRISIS
GETTING EVEN WITH THE ANSWERING MACHINE
ARE YOU A SPORTS NUT?
MEN ARE PIGS / WOMEN ARE BITCHES
THE BETTER HALF
ARE WE DYSFUNCTIONAL YET?
TECHNOLOGY BYTES!
50 WAYS TO HUSTLE YOUR FRIENDS
HORMONES FROM HELL
HUSBANDS FROM HELL
KILLER BRAS & Other Hazards Of The 50's
IT'S BETTER TO BE OVER THE HILL THAN UNDER IT
HOW TO REALLY PARTY!!!
WORK SUCKS!
THE PEOPLE WATCHER'S FIELD GUIDE
THE ABSOLUTE LAST CHANCE DIET BOOK
THE UGLY TRUTH ABOUT MEN
NEVER A DULL CARD
THE LITTLE BOOK OF ROMANTIC LIES

Retail $6.95
EVERYTHING I KNOW I LEARNED FROM TRASH TALK TV
IN A PERFECT WORLD
I WISH I DIDN'T...
THE TOILET ZONE
SIGNS / TOO MUCH TIME W/ CAT
LOVE & MARRIAGE & DIVORCE
CYBERGEEK IS CHIC
THE DIFFERENCE BETWEEN MEN AND WOMEN
GO TO HEALTH!
NOT TONIGHT, DEAR, I HAVE A COMPUTER!
THINGS YOU WILL NEVER HEAR THEM SAY
THE SENIOR CITIZENS'S SURVIVAL GUIDE
IT'S A MAD MAD MAD SPORTS WORLD
THE LITTLE BOOK OF CORPORATE LIES
RED HOT MONOGAMY
LOVE DAT CAT
HOW TO SURVIVE A JEWISH MOTHER

Retail $7.95
WHY MEN DON'T HAVE A CLUE
LADIES, START YOUR ENGINES!
ULI STEIN'S "ANIMAL LIFE"
ULI STEIN'S "I'VE GOT IT BUT IT'S JAMMED"
ULI STEIN'S "THAT SHOULD NEVER HAVE HAPPENED"

NO HANG-UPS – CASSETTES Retail $5.98

Vol. I:	GENERAL MESSAGES (M or F)
Vol. II:	BUSINESS MESSAGES (M or F)
Vol. III:	'R' RATED MESSAGES (M or F)
Vol. V:	CELEBRI-TEASE